A MAN'S REFLECTION

PETER EIKHUEMELO

ISBN 978-93-5883-057-6
© PETER EIKHUEMELO 2023

Published in India 2023 by Pencil

A brand of
One Point Six Technologies Pvt. Ltd.
Unit no. 26, Ground Floor, Building A1,
Wadala Truck Terminal Road,
Near Post Office, Antop Hill, Mumbai - 400037
E connect@thepencilapp.com
W www.thepencilapp.com

DISCLAIMER: *The opinions expressed in this book are those of the authors and do not purport to reflect the views of the Publisher.*

Author biography

A skilled author noted for his compelling storytelling and thought-provoking narratives is Peter Eikhuemelo. He has created a varied body of work that spans many genres, including fiction, romance, and contemporary literature, with a penchant for examining the complexities of human interactions and societal dynamics. Critical acclaim and a devoted readership have been attained as a result of their talent for developing engaging characters and exploring the depths of human emotions. He creates complex stories that connect with readers all across the world by drawing inspiration from his own experiences, cultural observations, and understanding of human nature. Their writings provide significant insights that encourage readers to consider the human condition, examine the complexities of love and identity, and challenge society's standards. By using evocative language and capturing the very essence.

CONTENTS

Introduction

The Reflections of a Man" is a timeless literary masterpiece that offers profound insights into the human experience. Written with remarkable introspection and eloquence, this book delves deep into the complexities of life, relationships, and self-discovery. Through a series of introspective reflections, the author takes readers on a transformative journey, exploring themes of love, growth, purpose, and the pursuit of happiness. With its poignant prose and relatable observations, "The Reflections of a Man" invites readers to contemplate their own lives, relationships, and aspirations. As the author aptly states, "In the depths of self-reflection, we uncover the truths that shape our existence and illuminate the path to our highest selves." Prepare to be captivated by the wisdom and depth of this extraordinary work as it resonates with the universal quest for understanding and fulfillment.

HUMANS FACTS

"Within each guy lies an untapped wellspring of potential, ready to be determined and harnessed. It is in embracing our strengths, overcoming our limitations, and embracing the journey of self-discovery that we unlock our true power. Remember, the measure of a man is not solely defined by his achievements, but by his character, resilience, and the positive impact he leaves on the world. Rise above self-doubt, embrace growth, and let your actions speak volumes. You can shape your destiny and inspire those around you. Embrace the truth that lies within: you are capable, you are worthy, and have the power to create a life of purpose and fulfillment."

MEN'S KNOWLEDGE

"Love is the foundation, but what men know in a relationship is the key to unlocking its true potential. It is through their understanding, empathy, and dedication that they nurture and strengthen the bond they share. What men know in a relationship goes beyond mere words or gestures; it is the profound wisdom that guides their actions, deepens their connection, and builds a love that withstands the test of time. So let us explore the depth of what men truly know in a relationship and uncover the transformative power it holds for both partners."

"What Men Know in a Relationship: Nurturing the Bonds of Love" In the realm of relationships, men possess a wealth of knowledge that helps them navigate the intricate dynamics of love, respect, and mutual understanding. What men know in a relationship reflects their commitment to fostering a deep connection, supporting their partner's growth, and building a foundation of trust and respect. Men know the significance of effective communication. They understand that open and honest dialogue is the lifeblood of a healthy relationship. They actively listen to their partners, seeking to understand their needs, desires, and concerns. They express themselves with sincerity and empathy, fostering an environment where both partners feel heard and valued. Men know the importance of emotional support. They recognize that love extends beyond grand gestures and romantic moments; it is in the small acts of kindness, comfort, and encouragement that a relationship thrives. They offer a safe space for their partners to express their emotions, providing unwavering support during both joys and challenges. Men know the power of compromise. They understand that relationships require mutual give and take. They navigate disagreements with grace and a willingness to find common ground, recognizing that the strength of a relationship lies in the ability to find solutions that honor both partners' needs and aspirations. Men realize the fee of accepting as true with fidelity. They recognize that trust is the cornerstone of a solid relationship. They remain faithful, both emotionally and physically, honoring the commitment they have made to their partner. They build trust through consistent honesty, reliability, and transparency.

Men know the importance of personal growth within a relationship. They understand that nurturing their own individuality is crucial for a healthy partnership. They encourage and support their partners' personal goals and dreams, celebrating their achievements and providing a source of unwavering encouragement.

Men know the significance of shared experiences and quality time. They create opportunities to strengthen the bond with their partner, whether through shared hobbies, adventures, or simply spending uninterrupted time together. They cherish these moments, knowing that the memories they create become the foundation of their shared journey.

Men know the power of forgiveness and understanding. They acknowledge that no relationship is without its flaws and missteps. They embrace forgiveness, seeking to understand their partner's perspective, and work together to overcome challenges and grow stronger as a couple.

In conclusion, what men know in a relationship reflects their dedication, empathy, and willingness to grow together. It is through their understanding, commitment, and continuous efforts that they cultivate a love that stands the test of time. Let us celebrate and embrace the wisdom men possess in relationships, as it holds the potential to transform love into an enduring and deeply fulfilling bond.

EGO OF A MAN

"Let love triumph as ego takes its humble bow."

A man's ego in affinity is a delicate balance between self-assurance and vulnerability. It is a powerful force that can shape the dynamics of a partnership. While a healthy level of confidence can inspire and provide a strong foundation, an unchecked ego can hinder communication, breed selfishness, and create distance. It is essential for a man to cultivate self-awareness, empathy, and humility to navigate the complexities of a relationship. By recognizing the needs and perspectives of their partner, setting aside pride, and embracing open communication, a man can foster a deep connection built on mutual respect, trust, and love. Nurturing a relationship requires the ability to put the ego aside, prioritize the happiness and well-being of both partners and create a harmonious and fulfilling bond.

SHOULD HE CHANGES IN FRONT OF HIS FRIENDS?

"True growth shines when he remains authentic, even amidst the influence of his friends, for love knows no masks".

When a man changes his behavior around his friends in a relationship, it can be a complex situation that requires open communication and understanding. While it's natural for individuals to adapt to different social environments, it's important for him to maintain authenticity and uphold the values and commitments of the relationship. Changes in behavior may stem from a desire to fit in or seek validation from his friends. In such cases, honest dialogue becomes crucial to address any discrepancies and ensure that both partners feel respected and supported. Building trust and mutual understanding allows for a healthy balance between personal identity and maintaining a strong partnership.

IF YOU ARE NOT INCLUDED

"If he doesn't include you, perhaps it's time to find someone who will."

In a relationship, feeling excluded can be a significant concern when your partner doesn't include you in various aspects of their life. It can lead to feelings of loneliness, insecurity, and a lack of emotional connection. It's important to communicate openly and honestly with your partner about your feelings and the importance of inclusion. Understanding their perspective and addressing any underlying issues is crucial. However, if the pattern persists and your needs for inclusion and involvement are consistently disregarded, it may be indicative of deeper compatibility issues. Remember, a healthy relationship should be built on mutual respect, support, and the desire to include and involve each other in all aspects of life.

TITLE OF BONDING "MY MAIN"

"My main, my love, forever intertwined in this beautiful journey."

In a relationship, the term "main" carries a special significance. It denotes a deep connection, loyalty, and commitment between partners. Being someone's "main" signifies that they hold a primary and cherished place in your heart and life. It represents a bond that surpasses any superficial or fleeting connection. Calling your partner "main" reflects a sense of exclusivity, trust, and dedication. It signifies a level of importance and priority, highlighting the deep emotional and romantic connection you share. This term serves as a reminder of the special role your partner plays in your life, symbolizing the love and devotion that forms the foundation of your relationship.

THE EVIL MAN

"The evil man may cross your path, but fear not, for he is but a stepping stone on the path to finding the one who will love and cherish you as you deserve."

It is a challenging and emotionally draining experience. It refers to being involved with someone who is incompatible, emotionally unavailable, or who exhibits behaviors that are detrimental to the health and happiness of the partnership. Being with the wrong man can lead to feelings of dissatisfaction, unfulfilled needs, and a sense of being trapped in a relationship that lacks the qualities necessary for a healthy and fulfilling connection.

One of the key indicators of being with the wrong man is a persistent feeling of incompatibility. You may find that your values, goals, or communication styles clash, leading to ongoing conflicts and a lack of harmony. The wrong man may also exhibit patterns of behavior such as dishonesty, lack of respect, or an inability to meet your emotional needs. These behaviors erode trust and create an imbalance within the relationship.

Recognizing that you are with the wrong man is an important step towards personal growth and finding a more suitable partner. It requires self-reflection, honesty, and the courage to make difficult decisions. Assessing your own needs, desires, and boundaries is crucial in determining whether the relationship aligns with your long-term happiness.

While being with the wrong man can be painful and disheartening, it can also serve as a valuable learning experience. It teaches you about your own worth, needs, and desires. It provides an opportunity for personal growth and a reevaluation of what you truly want and deserve in a relationship.

It is essential to prioritize your own well-being and consider what brings you genuine happiness and fulfillment. Recognize that you have the power to choose a partner who is supportive, loving, and compatible with you. Trust your instincts and have faith that the right man, who values and cherishes you, is out there.

Finally, being with the wrong man in a relationship can be a challenging and emotionally exhausting experience. It is important to recognize the signs of incompatibility and prioritize your own well-being. Remember that this experience is not a reflection of your worth, but rather an opportunity for personal growth and the eventual pursuit of a more fulfilling and harmonious relationship.

MR. WEAK

"A weak man finds strength in accepting his vulnerabilities, for it is through growth and resilience that he transforms weakness into unwavering strength."

In the context of a relationship, Mr. weak man refers to an individual who demonstrates a lack of emotional strength, maturity, and the ability to meet the needs of their partner effectively. A weak man may exhibit behaviors that undermine the foundation of a healthy and fulfilling partnership, such as insecurity, dependence, and an inability to provide emotional support. One of the key aspects of a weak man in a relationship is his emotional insecurity. He may frequently seek validation, reassurance, and approval from his partner, displaying a lack of confidence and self-assurance. This can create an imbalanced dynamic in the relationship, as his constant need for validation may place a burden on his partner and hinder their own emotional well-being. A weak man may also struggle with dependency, relying heavily on his partner for emotional stability and decision-making. This dependency can result in an unhealthy level of clinginess, possessiveness, and an inability to assert his own needs or desires. This can result in emotions of suffocation and resentment in the relationship. Furthermore, a weak man may struggle with providing emotional support to his partner. He may lack the empathy, understanding, and emotional maturity necessary to be a reliable source of comfort and encouragement. This can create an imbalance where his partner feels unsupported and emotionally neglected. It is important to note that being a weak man in a relationship is not a permanent state. With introspection, personal growth, and a commitment to change, a weak man can transform into a stronger, more supportive partner. Developing emotional strength and maturity requires cultivating self-awareness, embracing vulnerability, and actively working on communication and empathy skills. Seeking therapy or counseling can be instrumental in addressing underlying issues and developing healthier patterns of behavior. Ultimately, both partners in a relationship have a responsibility to support each other's emotional well-being. It is pivotal for Mr. Weak to acknowledge his shortcomings, take ownership of his actions, and commit to personal growth. By doing so, he can create a more balanced and fulfilling relationship, characterized by mutual support, understanding, and emotional resilience.

SOLITUDE VERSUS CONFIDENTIALITY

"In the depths of solitude, secrets find solace in trust."

Solitude and confidentiality play distinct but interconnected roles within a relationship. Solitude refers to the state of being alone or having personal space for introspection and self-reflection, while confidentiality pertains to the trust and privacy maintained in sharing sensitive or personal information. Solitude is essential for individuals to nurture their own sense of self, recharge, and foster personal growth. It allows for introspection, self-discovery, and the exploration of individual interests and passions. Solitude can be a time of rejuvenation, where one can reflect on their thoughts, feelings, and desires, ultimately enhancing self-awareness and emotional well-being. Confidentiality, on the other hand, is an integral aspect of trust in a relationship. It involves respecting and honoring the privacy of each partner and maintaining the trust placed in the sharing of personal experiences, emotions, and vulnerabilities. Privacy creates a safe and supportive space for open communication, where both partners feel secure in sharing their deepest thoughts and feelings without fear of judgment or betrayal. While solitude and confidentiality are distinct concepts, they intertwine in a relationship. Solitude allows individuals to process their thoughts and emotions, helping them communicate their needs more effectively when they come together. By engaging in healthy self-reflection during moments of solitude, individuals can gain clarity and better understand their own desires and boundaries, which they can then communicate confidentially within the relationship. Confidentiality also supports solitude, as it fosters an environment where partners can openly express themselves without fear of their personal information being divulged or used against them. Knowing that their confidential discussions will be respected cultivates a sense of security, which encourages individuals to be more open and vulnerable within the relationship. Balancing solitude and confidentiality demand effective communication and understanding. Each partner should recognize and respect the need for personal space and time for solitude, while also upholding the importance of confidentiality when sharing intimate thoughts and experiences. Open discussions about boundaries and expectations regarding privacy and confidentiality can help establish a strong foundation of trust and mutual respect. In the end, solitude and confidentiality are interconnected elements in a relationship. Solitude provides individuals with valuable self-reflection and personal growth, while confidentiality builds trust and fosters a safe space for open communication. Balancing these aspects allows for the cultivation of individual well-being and the development of a strong, intimate connection within the affinity.

TRUST

"Trust: the cornerstone of love, the fuel that ignites souls."

Trust is a fundamental pillar of any strong and healthy relationship. It is the bulwark upon which love, intimacy, and emotional connection are built. Trust enables individuals to feel safe, secure, and confident in their relationship, knowing that their partner has their best interests at heart. It establishes a sense of reliability, dependability, and mutual respect. In a relationship, trust goes beyond mere belief or faith; it is earned and nurtured through consistent actions, transparency, and open communication. Trust requires vulnerability, as it involves letting down one's guard and allowing oneself to be seen and accepted for who they truly are. When trust is present, it creates a strong sense of emotional safety. Partners can confide in each other, share their deepest fears and desires, and seek support without the fear of judgment or betrayal. Trust allows for open and honest communication, fostering an environment where both partners can express their feelings, needs, and concerns without reservation. Trust also acts as a protective shield against insecurities and doubts. When trust is established, individuals feel confident in their partner's loyalty and commitment. They can rely on their partner's words and actions, knowing that they will follow through on their promises and be there in times of need. Trust allows couples to build a solid foundation of mutual support, understanding, and respect. However, trust is delicate and can be easily broken. Betrayal, dishonesty, or inconsistent behavior can erode trust, creating fractures in the relationship. Rebuilding trust requires time, effort, and a willingness to address the underlying issues that led to its breakdown. It involves sincere apologies, accountability, and demonstrating through actions that one has learned from past mistakes. Rebuilding trust is a joint effort that requires patience, forgiveness, and a commitment to open and transparent communication. Finally, trust is an essential element in a relationship. It provides the emotional safety and security necessary for love and intimacy to flourish. Nurturing trust involves consistent actions, open communication, and the willingness to be vulnerable. When trust is present, it creates a strong foundation for a healthy, fulfilling, and lasting relationship.

INFIDELITY

"Healing the wounds of infidelity with love's resilient embrace"

Throughout the history of romantic relationships, people have been fascinated by, thoughtful about, and troubled by the timeless and tragic subject of infidelity. It is characterized as the betrayal of trust and loyalty in a love relationship and strikes at the very heart of our emotional ties. Infidelity crosses the boundaries of time and culture, leaving a path of broken vows, illusions, and heartbreak in its wake. Infidelity has been used as an intriguing narrative device throughout literature, from the classic works of Shakespeare and Tolstoy to the earliest tales of Greek mythology, reflecting the complexity and frailties of human nature.

The violation of the implicit or explicit commitment between two people to protect the exclusivity and sanctity of their partnership constitutes the essence of infidelity. It appears in a variety of ways, encompasses treachery on both a physical and emotional level. Indulging in temptation, desire, or a need for novelty, the unfaithful partner may look for comfort or thrill in the arms of another. The foundation of trust is undermined by this act, leaving the betrayed partner adrift in a sea of uncertainty, suffering, and self-doubt.

Infidelity has been studied from a variety of angles throughout history. Philosophers ponder the ethical ramifications, psychologists explore the psychological drivers, and sociologists assess the effects on society as a whole. It is a universal occurrence that is unconstrained by socioeconomic class, gender, or age. Infidelity permeates every aspect of our lives, from the high-profile incidents involving famous people to the covert affairs of regular people.

After a cheating partner, the encompasses treachery on both a physical and emotional level. Indulging in temptation, desire, or a need for novelty, the unfaithful partner may look for comfort or thrill in the arms of another. The foundation of trust is undermined by this act, leaving the betrayed partner adrift in a sea of uncertainty, suffering, and self-doubt. After a cheating partner, the spouse who has been betrayed goes through a wide range of emotions. They struggle with strong emotions of grief, hurt, and rage. Their spirit is gnawed by the feeling of betrayal, creating wounds that might never fully recover. Once shattered, trust is a delicate commodity that takes a lot of work to repair. The effects of infidelity are extensive. Relationships may either break down under the weight of betrayed trust or go through a healing process that is transformative. The road to healing necessitates vulnerability, open and honest conversation, and introspection. Couples may start therapy or counseling journeys in search of direction and help to navigate the perilous rivers of emotional turbulence.

Infidelity continues to enchant audiences in literature and the arts. It explores themes of human weakness and acts as a metaphor for human weakness, looking at themes like desire, temptation, and the tension between passion and duty. These tales, which range from Anna Karenina's sad affair to Madame Bovary's tortured love triangle, shed light on the nuanced intricacies of human relationships and the repercussions of deviating from the road of faithfulness.

Infidelity is a perennial and extraordinarily intricate aspect of human relationships, to sum up. It brings up strong feelings, makes us question our moral compass, and makes our shared path of love and commitment vulnerable. The study of infidelity serves as both a warning and a mirror to our own experiences, reminding us of the delicate balance needed to protect and maintain the relationships that are most important to us.

DOUBLE CHANCE

"Relationships are like melodies; they can falter at times, but given another chance, they can come together to form a symphony of love and development."

Relationships are intricate and dynamic relationships between people that are marked by affection, trust, and understanding. Even the most happy partnerships, though, occasionally run into roadblocks and difficulties. When these difficulties result in a relationship's dissolution, the idea of a "second chance" frequently appears as a possible route for healing and development.

A second chance in a relationship is the chance for two people to get back together after some time apart or conflict. It represents a readiness to repair any harm done to the foundation of love and trust as well as a desire to forgive. Giving someone a second opportunity can be a life-changing experience for both parties, albeit it depends on the situation and the people involved. Introspection and personal development are important components of second chances. Understanding the root causes of the relationship's decline is essential. It necessitates an open assessment of one's own behavior and inadequacies, as well as comprehension of the partner's viewpoint. Self-reflection enables people to accept accountability for their actions, grow personally, and learn from their mistakes.

Introspection and personal development are important components of second chances. Understanding the root causes of the relationship's decline is essential. It necessitates an open assessment of one's own behavior and inadequacies, as well as comprehension of the partner's viewpoint. Self-reflection enables people to accept accountability for their actions, grow personally, and learn from their mistakes.

In the process of giving someone a second chance, communication is essential. Both partners can share their feelings, worries, and expectations through an honest and open conversation. Empathy and active listening promote comprehension, which makes it easier to regain trust. It takes time to repair the relationship's emotional links and foundations, thus this process calls for patience.

Second chances are built on the foundation of forgiveness. It entails putting the past wounds and grudges behind us and looking forward to a future based on mutual respect and trust. Although it is difficult, forgiveness can open up opportunities for healing and development. Moving forward without harboring resentments or regrets from the past demands a sincere commitment.

In summary, revisits in relationships provide couples a chance to mend fences, heal wounds, and strengthen their bond. Couples can engage on a converting path towards a healthier and more fulfilling connection via reflection, communication, forgiving one another, and building trust. But it's vital to keep in mind that not all relationships are meant to be saved, and sometimes it's preferable for both parties to move on individually.

UNTEACHABLE

"The most important lessons are frequently learned in a relationship's unteachable moments, despite the fact that love is a profound teacher."

Being "unteachable" has significant implications in the complex web of relationships. Although traditional education involves planned instruction and purposeful direction, the most important relationship lessons can come from unteachable times. These instances go beyond textbooks and lesson plans, developing in the unfiltered and uncontrollable world of feelings, encounters, and communal vulnerability.

The invisible nuances and spontaneous exchanges that mold our perception of love, trust, and progress are the unteachable part of a relationship. People discover the most about themselves, their partners, and the complexities of human connection in these unexplored areas. In this world, the heart serves as the compass and real-world encounters serve as the curriculum.

Being unteachable in this situation entails a readiness to let go of inflexible expectations and preconceived conceptions. It entails letting go of the notion that we are in charge of a relationship's trajectory or that we have all the solutions. As a substitute, it challenges us to embrace the unknowable and to be receptive to the unexpected teachings that come up naturally and organically.

The unteachable moments frequently result from disagreements and difficulties that put a partnership to the test. They could result from bitter betrayals, misunderstandings, or even conflicts. These situations may make people feel uncomfortable and may test their limitations. However, the discomfort offers a chance for development and change. True sensitivity shows itself in these teachable times. Walls come down, exposing the true, unadulterated parts of who we are. We face our worries, insecurities, and faults in this setting. We are taught the value of compassion, empathy, and active listening. We come to understand the need of forgiving ourselves as well as our relationships.

Fortitude is also fostered by unteachable moments. They show us that although partnerships are not immune to difficulties, it is our capacity to overcome them that makes the connection stronger. These times require unflinching devotion, tolerance, and patience. They serve as a reminder that love is a journey, not a destination, where learning and progress are entwined.

Beyond personal development, the unlearnable lessons also foster the relationship's overall development. Partners develop better communication skills and learn how to resolve disputes amicably and empathetically. They gain the ability to embrace vulnerability and foster an environment that is free from judgment. They learn the value of togetherness and the beauty of compromise.

One must adopt a humble and inquisitive mindset if they want to completely enjoy the unteachable times. It calls for an acceptance of the fact that we are always learners in the school of love and that real knowledge comes from realizing the size of what we don't know. We become open to the profound teachings that emerge spontaneously in the ebb and flow of a relationship when we let go of the urge to be the teacher.

In a relationship, being "unteachable" entails accepting the lessons that come up outside of formal instruction. People learn more about themselves, their partners, and the complexities of human connection via unscripted moments of vulnerability, conflict, and progress. Individuals develop courage , empathy, and unity by letting go of preconceived ideas and welcoming the unknown, fostering a connection that thrives on ongoing learning and development.

PAID TIME

"Every moment spent together is an investment and paid time in a relationship is the most valuable currency.

Time is a precious resource amid the hectic complexity of modern life. "Paid time" in the context of relationships refers to the consciously chosen expenditure of special times with our loved ones. It represents the deliberate decision to give our relationship with one another top priority and set aside specific time to do so. Paid time is being emotionally and intellectually totally present with our partner, going beyond only being physically present. It entails eliminating distractions, cutting off from technology, and fostering an atmosphere that fosters genuine connection. These interactions lay the groundwork for a long-lasting and fulfilling relationship.

Paid time is fundamentally about having shared experiences. Participating in activities in a group offers chances for friendship, hilarity, and the making of enduring memories. Adventures, indulgence in common interests, or even just enjoying a meal together all promote a sense of closeness and strengthen the emotional bond between spouses.

Paid time must also include effective communication. Both spouses can share their ideas, emotions, and aspirations by setting aside time for meaningful interactions. It gives people a place to actively listen, validate one another's experiences, and encourage one another through both successes and setbacks. These open channels of communication strengthen the relationship's basis by fostering emotional connection and building trust. Paid time also need affection and gratitude. Small acts of love and appreciation, like holding hands, snuggling, or expressing gratitude, show our spouse how much we care about them. These deeds of compassion and affection show how much we cherish having them in our lives. We cultivate a secure and supportive environment where love can blossom by regularly showing affection.

Additionally, paid time involves getting to know one another's interests and goals. It entails actively contributing to our partner's development. We promote a sense of support and encouragement by showing sincere interest in their interests, objectives, and aspirations. The connection is strengthened by this shared commitment to one another's personal development, which demonstrates a strong desire for our loved one to be happy and fulfilled.

Finding paid time can be difficult because of the pressures of daily life, but it is important to prioritize it and make an effort to make room for it. Setting limits, controlling timetables, and finding concessions might be necessary for this. The benefits, nevertheless, are enormous. By investing in paid time, we show our spouse that we are committed to the relationship and are making them a top priority in our lives.

In result, investing quality time with our loved ones is what we mean when we say that relationships require paid time. It includes having common interests and experiences with one another as well as having good communication skills, affection, and support for one another. We may enhance the relationship, foster emotional connection, and create a stronger relationship by making a conscious effort to prioritize and allocate focused time.

PERSISTENCE

"Persistence: the unyielding dedication to face challenges, withstand calamities, and fan the flame of love in the journey of relationships."

Persistence appears in the web of relationships as a staunch and unyielding dedication to connection and love. It is the tenacious flame that endures the rigors of time and struggle, promoting development, comprehension, and strong emotional ties. Persistence emerges as the driving force that pulls couples onward in the face of difficulties and challenges, enabling them to surmount adversities and grow their love.

True perseverance goes beyond simple endurance; it involves making a conscious decision to fight for the connection even when the going gets tough. It exemplifies the willingness to exert the work and commitment necessary to successfully negotiate the complexity of human connection. Even in the face of conflicts, misunderstandings, or disappointments, it is a daily practice to choose love.

A strong belief in the possibilities of the connection is at the heart of persistence. It is the conviction that the shared love is valuable enough to put effort into, such as time, energy, and emotional vulnerability. A shared future vision, a shared commitment to development, and reciprocal support are the foundations of persistence. It acknowledges that connections change through time and that true fulfillment comes from making an effort to build a relationship that endures.

Persistence in the face of obstacles shows up as frank and open conversation. It is a dedication to hearing and comprehending others while looking for areas of agreement between divergent viewpoints. Recognizing that disagreements will inevitably arise but yet seeing them as opportunities for further learning

Persistence ultimately serves as a moving example of the strength of love and human connection. To endure adversity, conquer challenges, and maintain the flame of love requires intentional choice. It stands for the dedication to supporting one another through difficult times and cooperating to develop a relationship that is strong, contenting, and enduring.

In the final analysis, maintaining relationships entails a firm commitment and deliberate work to foster love and kinship. To persevere in the face of obstacles, disagreements, and disappointments is a decision. Couples who maintain their love lay the groundwork for development, comprehension, and intense emotional relationships by being open with one another, forgiving one another, and showing resiliency. Perseverance is the key to building relationships that endure difficulties.

Additionally, forgiveness and the capacity to move past hurts are parts of persistence. It recognizes that flaws and errors can occur in every connection. Release of resentment and selection of compassion and understanding as a substitute are choices. Giving room for development and rebirth within the relationship, forgiveness promotes healing. Couples can regain trust and go on together by forgiving one another.

Resilience is fostered by maintaining relationships. It understands that obstacles and struggles are a necessary element of the trip but do not sum up the entire narrative. Instead, they offer chances for development and change. Resilient couples understand that obstacles can serve as stepping stones that help them grow as people and as a couple by learning from them, adapting, and moving on.

The appeal of "Now is your turn" requires us to sincerely perform loving and good deeds. It entails being aware of, receptive to, and present to one's partner's wants and desires. It is a purposeful decision to pay close attention, comprehend completely, and offer unflinching support. These altruistic deeds deepen the ties of closeness and trust, laying the groundwork for a relationship that will develop.

NOW IS YOUR TURN

"It's your turn now. Seize the chance to love, to give, and to build the lovely tale of our relationship together."

The adage "Now is your turn" delivers a powerful message in the world of relationships, asking people to seize the chance to love, give, and actively participate in the lovely story of their relationship. It denotes a change in perspective, a time when one partner realizes the significance of their contribution to the growth of love, understanding, and harmony.

"Now is your turn" is a gentle reminder that each partner has the ability to develop and influence the relationship. It is a call to action. It recognizes that relationships are active, ongoing journeys that demand deliberate effort and attention rather than being passive pursuits. It represents a crucial turning point when someone realizes their ability to change things and make a contribution to the world.

The appeal of "Now is your turn" requires us to sincerely perform loving and good deeds. It entails being aware of, receptive to, and present to one's partner's wants and desires. It is a purposeful decision to pay close attention, comprehend completely, and offer unflinching support. These altruistic deeds deepen the ties of closeness and trust, laying the groundwork for a relationship that will develop.

The phrase "Now is your turn" also captures the idea of balance and reciprocity in a relationship. It acknowledges the fact that love is a two-way street and that both parties are accountable for fostering the relationship. Being invited to alternate between giving and receiving serves as a reminder that love is about more than just keeping score. Additionally, "Now is your turn" promotes introspection and personal development. It encourages people to reflect on themselves, evaluate their own actions, and make an effort to better themselves. It is an invitation to take responsibility for one's behaviors and acknowledge the effect they have on the relationship. People foster an environment that fosters the growth of the relationship itself when they take ownership of their own personal development.

At its essence, "Now is your turn" emphasizes the power of love, reminding listeners that they have the power to influence both their own and their partner's happiness. It challenges individuals to face their fears and vulnerabilities, embrace their vulnerability, and fully appreciate the beauty of a shared journey. It represents a chance to co-write a story that is joyful.

Lastly, the phrase "Now is your turn" in a relationship denotes a crucial time for awareness and action. It exhorts people to actively partake in loving, kind, and understanding deeds. It focuses on the significance of reciprocity, balance, and personal development in fostering an amicable relationship. By responding to the call of "Now is your turn," people foster a climate of love, trust, and support for one another, which enables the relationship to grow and flourish.

THE TERROR OF RESETTLE

"The anxiety of beginning over, but also the bravery to embrace the unknown and rebuild love from the ashes "

The expression "the terror of resettle" captures the great fear and uncertainty that develop when forced to start over in the complex web of ties. To face the unknown and resurrect love from the ashes is a terrifying path that calls for extraordinary bravery. The possibility for development, change, and the discovery of a love that is more powerful and resilient than ever before, however, resides within this horror.

The ability to communicate becomes crucial for overcoming the anxiety of relocation. It calls for frank conversation in which both parties can voice their emotions, worries, and future aspirations. Building a foundation of trust via open and honest communication makes it possible to explore common values, objectives, and aspirations. A new vision for the partnership that is based on a stronger, more genuine connection can develop through these discussions.

On the journey of resettlement, patience and resiliency are essential allies. It takes time to rebuild a relationship, and obstacles may appear along the road. It is imperative to possess the patience necessary to allow for natural healing to take place and to give the relationship the room it requires to develop. It takes resiliency to handle the

In times of significant change or turbulence in a relationship, the anxiety of resettle manifests. Events like a breakup, a betrayal, or a significant loss could set it off. The relationship's familiar foundation cracks, leaving a But in the face of this horror, a chance for fundamental development and rebirth presents itself. It is a plea to find the strength to face the unknowable, the suffering, and the unpredictability, and to set out on a journey to rebuild love from the rubble. It requires people to muster the courage to face their vulnerabilities, admit their hurts, and reopen their hearts. Introspection and self-reflection are necessary if one is to rebuild love in the face of the horror of resettlement. It encourages people to explore their deepest wants, anxieties, and vulnerabilities. It presents an opportunity to learn more about oneself and the part they performed in the previous relationship. Through self-awareness, people can take lessons from their history in the face of the fear of relocation, it's critical to keep in mind that the road to rebuilding is about working together to create a new future rather than trying to recreate the past. It is a chance to establish a bond that is more sincere, compatible with personal development, and durable. People can find a love that is developed through the strength to face uncertainty, to heal, and to rise stronger than ever before by embracing the terror of resettle.

In conclusion, the fear of beginning over in partnerships symbolizes a difficult road. To face the unknown and restore love from the ashes takes tremendous courage. This is a moment for reflection, honest dialogue, tolerance, and fortitude. By accepting the fear of.

PERFECT, POWERFUL WOMAN

"The ideal woman is a timeless example of power, grace, and love who pushes her lover to new heights."

In a relationship, the idea of the "perfect, powerful woman" captures the traditional vision of femininity as a harmonic synthesis of power, grace, and love. She is a timeless archetype that uplifts and encourages her partner, fostering a dynamic relationship based on respect, personal development, and deep connection.

The alluring presence of the perfect, strong woman comes from her inner fortitude. She exudes confidence and resiliency because she has a strong sense of self-belief in her talents. Her strength is a gentle force that gives the partnership a strong foundation rather than being overbearing or domineering. It gives her partner the freedom to be themselves, to value their own assets, and to pursue personal development with her.

The perfect, strong woman has a disposition that is characterized by grace. She has a polished posture that mesmerizes everyone around her as she carries herself with grace and respect. Her grace is evident in her behaviors, words, and interactions with those inside the relationship in addition to her outward attractiveness. She approaches challenging situations with coolness and sensitivity, navigating difficulties and disagreements with insight and tact. Her elegance fosters harmony and open communication by building an environment of respect and understanding.

The flawless, strong woman exudes love with ease. She has a rich reservoir of empathy, generosity, and compassion that she freely shares with her spouse. She accepts her spouse for who they are and supports their development and ambitions with unwavering affection. Through her tender actions, uplifting words, and steadfast support The ideal, strong woman is dedicated to and committed to her role as a partner. She respects the sanctity of the union and is aware of its importance in their life. She is the epitome of fidelity, loyalty, and the determination to support her lover no matter what. Her continuous support fosters a climate of security and trust in the union, enabling both partners to be completely honest and open about their weaknesses.

In the traditional sense, the ideal, strong woman encourages her partner to become their best selves. She supports their aspirations, promotes their personal development, and acknowledges their accomplishments. Instead of feeling frightened by their success, she savors it as if it were her own. The catalyst is her unshakeable faith in her partner's potential. The ideal, strong woman in a relationship exemplifies time-tested traits that support a happy and meaningful connection. She acts as a beacon of hope, encouraging both spouses to play to their strengths, cherish their love, and foster a feeling of meaning and fulfillment in their union. Her classic representation raises the relationship to new heights of happiness, comprehension, and harmony by serving as a reminder of the transformative power of love, grace, and inner strength.

In the final analysis, the ideal, strong woman in a relationship embodies the traditional ideals of courage, beauty, and affection. She radiates unwavering love, grace, and elegance. She is the embodiment of inner power. Her presence motivates and uplifts her companion, building a strong bond based on appreciation and personal development. The ideal, acts as strong lady.

A NEW LEVEL BEING SET

"Embrace the ability to rewrite the rules of love, establishing a connection that transcends expectations and motivates others to strive for more."

In partnerships, the expression "a new level being set" captures the deeper essence of development, evolution, and a strengthening bond between partners. It denotes a motivational turning point in the course of love, where the two people raise their connection above and beyond preconceived notions and constraints.

Setting a new level in a partnership signifies a shared dedication to improvement and growth. We both agree that love is a dynamic energy that changes and grows with time rather than being static. This common commitment is the basis for the transformation that takes place, propelling the partnership to new heights. Making the decision to promote personal development is the first step in raising the bar in a partnership. In an effort to better understand who they are and connect their values and objectives, both people set out on a voyage of introspection. To bring their most genuine selves to the partnership, they actively strive to improve themselves by always learning and growing. Fostering frank and open dialogue is a necessary part of accepting a new level. It involves providing a safe environment where both partners may freely communicate their needs, wants, and vulnerabilities. They develop a deeper understanding of one another through real and kind communication, strengthening their emotional bond. They can manage difficulties and disagreements with grace and understanding because of this degree of communication, which serves as the foundation of trust. Extending the comfort zone and engaging in novel experiences as a couple is frequently necessary to take a relationship to the next level. It entails embracing novelty, venturing outside of the comfort zone, and taking measured risks that foster shared joy and growth. As they weave a tapestry of shared experiences and learn new things about themselves and their relationship, the partners' exploration voyage deepens their bond.

Along with increased intimacy and emotional connection, a new level is being established. It is a dedication to openness in which both partners consent to being deeply seen and known. They create an environment where people may express their deepest fears, hopes, and desires, leading to a strong emotional bond. They can help one another because of their level of intimacy. Setting a new standard in a relationship includes inspiring others. Partners inspire people around them by setting an example of growth, resiliency, and genuine connection. Their union serves as an example of what may happen when love is cultivated with purpose and commitment. They inspire people to seek out deeper connections and to raise the bar in their own relationships by their example.

Setting a new level in a relationship, then, symbolizes an energizing path of development, kinship, and transformation on both sides. It necessitates a dedication to one's own development, as well as open conversation, exploration, and increasing intimacy. By choosing this route, partners forge a closeness that goes above and beyond expectations, motivating one another and others to aim higher and cultivate relationships that endure.

WHO IS FOR YOU

"Embrace the one on the journey of love whose presence ignites your soul, nurtures your development, and loves you without condition."

Relationship experts agree that the question "Who is for you?" captures the spirit of discovering the one person who is destined to be our partner on our romantic journey. It asks us to consider the characteristics and dynamics that characterize a meaningful relationship, highlighting the significance of an enduring bond based on love, development, and mutual support.

We set out to find a soulmate—a companion whose presence profoundly enriches our lives—when we ask the question, "Who is for you?" in relationships. It goes beyond merely being compatible and visually attractive. Finding someone whose energy is compatible with ours and whose ideals and objectives are in line with our own is all about finding that person. The person who sincerely supports you is a source of motivation and inspiration. They inspire and enable us to realize our greatest potential while pushing us to advance both personally and collectively. They are our unwavering ally, encouraging us to go higher and pursue excellence while also providing unshakable support and faith in our dreams. We feel seen, heard, and accepted for who we really are when they are around. Through shared ideals and a mutual comprehension of each other's wants and ambitions, an everlasting relationship is created. It is based on a foundation of open communication, honesty, and trust. A confidant is someone with whom you can discuss your innermost feelings, anxieties, and weaknesses.

Love flows freely and unreservedly in this enduring connection. It is a love that endures the rigors of life and the passage of time. It is based on a strong emotional connection that develops over time rather than a momentary passion alone. You can find comfort, understanding, and acceptance in the unshakable, lasting love of the one who is for you.

We feel a sense of fulfillment and belonging when we find the one who is for us. In the face of life's difficulties, their presence becomes a pillar of support. Together, we experience the highs and lows, cherishing happy times and seeking comfort in their presence during difficult ones.

In ending, the question "Who is for you?" encourages us to look for a lasting connection that goes beyond outward appearances of compatibility and appeal. It motivates us to look for a soul mate—someone who encourages us to develop, loves us ardently, and supports us without conditions. We have a deep sense of fulfillment, friendship, and belonging through this relationship. Accepting the person who actually cares for us results in enduring love, forging a relationship that endures the test of time and fosters our development along the path of love.

THINKING ABOUT

"Thinking about the needs, desires, and dreams of our loved ones opens the door to deeper understanding, connection, and an extraordinary journey together, paving the path to true growth in relationships."

One of the most meaningful actions we may take in the area of relationships is the practice of "thinking about." It is an intentional and conscious process that goes beyond the surface level and directs us to greater empathy, understanding, and connections with others we care about.

Thinking about someone entails going beyond simple consideration and delving deeply into the complex web of their ideas, feelings, and motivations. It requires sincere interest and a sincere effort to understand the subtleties of their existence. It demands us to temporarily put our own concerns aside and give our full attention to the person in front of us.

It is simple to become mired in our own internal whirlwinds of ideas, obligations, and aspirations in the busy turmoil of our life. The small changes in the behavior of those who are closest to us—their unsaid concerns, their concealed goals, and their silent cries for connection—can be overlooked unwittingly. But if we choose to carefully consider them, we learn to hear the symphony of their silent hearts, which enables us to respond to them with kindness and compassion.

To think about someone, we must imagine ourselves in their position, travel through their experiences, and recognize the many different viewpoints that have shaped their worldview. It entails accepting vulnerability because true insight can only be formed in the presence of vulnerability. By allowing ourselves to be open to their victories, sufferings, and pleasures Additionally, thinking about someone extends beyond the present. It is a commitment to the development and health of our relationships as well as an investment in the future. It entails imagining their hopes and dreams, assisting them in pursuing happiness, and lending a steady hand when difficulties emerge. When we actively consider our loved ones, we take on the roles of their unshakable supporters, defenders, and confidants.

Thinking about someone weaves the delicate thread of closeness and understanding into the tapestry of relationships. It changes casual chats into profound talks, passing conversations into lifetime friendships, and everyday events into unforgettable memories. It cultivates a haven for unconditional love, respect, and trust to grow.

Additionally, thinking about someone extends beyond the present. It is a commitment to the development and health of our relationships as well as an investment in the future. It entails imagining their hopes and dreams, assisting them in pursuing happiness, and lending a steady hand when difficulties emerge. When we actively consider our loved ones, we take on the roles of their unshakable supporters, defenders, and confidants.

Thinking about someone weaves the delicate thread of closeness and understanding into the tapestry of relationships. It changes casual chats into profound talks, passing conversations into lifetime friendships, and everyday events into unforgettable memories. It cultivates a safe haven for unconditional love, respect, and trust to grow.

Let's start doing this fantastic thing of thinking about one another. Let's celebrate the elegance of sympathy, the strength of comprehension, and the power of connection. May we take the time to appreciate the priceless people who bless our lives by actually seeing them, being seen by them, listening to them, and loving them. We build lasting relationships—relationships that enhance our lives and fill the world with love, compassion, and limitless joy—through the deep act of thinking about.

A WISE MAN

"A wise man deals with relationship with the compass of understanding, the rudder of empathy, and the sails of patience, steering towards the shores of harmonious connection and long-lasting fulfillment."

A wise guy serves as an anchor of knowledge, an example of emotional intelligence, and a person of great insight in the vast fabric of connections. His presence serves as a beacon, illuminating the way to peaceful relationships and fostering ties that last the test of time. A smart guy enters partnerships with a clear understanding of the complex dynamics at work. He comprehends that every person is a special mix of hopes, anxieties, dreams, and insecurities. With this understanding, he accepts the duty of exercising caution and attending to the minute details that mold the relationships he creates. The wise man immerses himself in other people's experiences through exhibiting empathy. He offers consolation during difficult times and joy during victories while listening with an open heart and focused attention. His remarks are filled with true compassion, are laced with kindness, and bear the weight of consideration. He is aware that genuine comprehension does not result from judgment but rather from a readiness to look past outward manifestations and grasp the depths of another person's soul. His approach to relationships is guided by the patience he values so much. He is aware that development requires time, that recovery is a process, and that deep connections need to be nurtured. He maintains his composure in the face of difficulty, enduring storms with unyielding resolution. His tolerance serves as a salve, healing scars, and A wise guy uses words with grace and tact, understanding the importance of communication. He is aware that effective communication involves more than just speaking; it also needs the ability to actively listen, interpret nonverbal cues, and recognize the unspoken. He values open communication in which respect and honesty coexist peacefully. He creates an atmosphere where trust can grow, and hearts can unite through open and honest communication.

The wise guy uses insight to help him balance commitment and freedom as he moves through the ups and downs of relationships. He understands the value of encouraging personal development while also looking out for the partnership's overall well-being. He is aware that love is a garden, not a prison, where both partners can grow.

The wise man is a timeless representation of emotional maturity and meaningful connection in a society that is frequently ruled by transient ambitions and rapid fulfillment. He serves as a reminder of the depth and beauty that relationships can possess when they are steered by wisdom, understanding, tolerance, and open communication. He motivates us to build remarkable connections, where hearts entwine, souls are fed, and love serves as an everlasting light of hope, by serving as an example.

A MAN TO ANOTHER MAN

"Let our hearts come together in understanding, let our actions speak truth, let our ties strengthen us to become the best versions of ourselves."

There is a holy kinship between men that transcends cordial bonds and reaches the depths of brotherhood inside the complex web of interactions. A remarkable journey of shared understanding, development, and support starts when one man extends his hand to another.

To another guy, a man represents strength—not only physical prowess but also resiliency that emanates from the very center of his existence. He is aware of the internal conflicts, obstacles overcome, and victories that mold a man's character. He provides a secure refuge where vulnerability is accepted and understood with understanding and compassion. Honesty becomes a pillar of this special relationship. The rawness of a guy's emotions, his worries, and his aspirations are revealed when he speaks his truths to another man. They create an unshakable kinship in this place of honesty. They encourage one another to tackle life's obstacles head-on, to face their inner demons, and to come out stronger on the other side through open communication. A man can easily show compassion to another man. He is aware of the pressure placed on individuals by social norms and the masks used to hide vulnerability. He gently reaches out to his neighbor, letting him know that he is not the only one going through this. He transforms into a ray of light at bad times, leading his counterpart toward self-acceptance, healing, and personal The power of accountability is embraced by a man to another man. He encourages his friend to fulfill his potential, keep his word, and hold himself to a higher standard. They encourage one another to excellence in this dance of shared accountability, never letting mediocrity define their journeys. Through unshakable loyalty, they serve as change agents.

A man to another man finds in this sacred connection a loyal ally, a rock-solid comrade who lifts him up in times of failure and serves as a constant reminder of his intrinsic value. They build a tapestry of memories via their shared experiences, which becomes the foundation of their relationship. A man to another man turns into a compass as they travel through life together. They support one another in their pursuit of honesty, integrity, and a sense of purpose. By setting a positive example, they encourage younger generations to reject conventional norms, redefine what it means to be a man, and develop connections based on respect, trust, and vulnerability.

So, let's respect the sacred bond that exists between males, a bond built on power, integrity, empathy, and responsibility. By redefining masculinity as a group, we may leave a lasting legacy of fraternity. Let us encourage, boost, and support one another as we embark on this enduring journey of personal growth.

HER LIMIT IS SET

"In the world of relationships, her potential is only limited by her capacity for dreaming big, for perseverance, and for unshakeable self-belief. Together, let's smash down barriers, challenge conventions, and give her the tools she needs to soar to unfathomable heights of love, joy, and fulfillment."

The idea that "her limit is set" has a significant meaning in the beautiful weaving of relationships. It embodies the notion that a woman's potential, development, and pleasure are not constrained by her environment or societal norms. Instead, the extent of her perseverance, inner strength, and steadfast self-confidence serve as her limit.

It is crucial to disrupt the current quo and knock down the barriers that prevent women from reaching their full potential in a world that frequently places restrictions and prohibitions on them. In relationships, it becomes everyone's obligation to create a space where she may thrive, free from society pressures or archaic conventions. Her limit is not determined by the uncertainties that nag at her or the judgments that try to keep her soul in check. Instead, it is created by her unwavering determination to conquer challenges, unshakable daring to dream, and reluctance to accept anything less than what her heart truly desires. These traits must be valued in a relationship in order to develop her dreams and assist her on her self-discovery path. The appeal of a happy relationship is found in the common conviction that her potential is limitless. It is a recognition that each person possesses the key to releasing the other's latent potential and sparking the flame of possibility within each of their souls. Together, they act as growth-promoting catalysts, encouraging one another to We have a responsibility as partners to be her steadfast pillars of strength and unrelenting advocates. We must create an atmosphere where she may openly communicate her ideas, feelings, and goals without worrying about criticism or retaliation. We can magnify her voice by paying close attention to what she has to say and appreciating it, which will inspire her to go beyond cultural norms and break through the barriers that are holding her back. We must accept that her limit may change throughout this voyage. As she develops, learns, and embraces her inner strength, she may be able to overcome what once seemed impossible. It is our duty to change and grow with her, to rejoice in her victories, and to negotiate the difficulties that come with each new chapter. Let's work together to establish a fair partnership that will serve as a safe haven for her to follow her aspirations, explore her passions, and develop into the best version of herself. Let's create an atmosphere that feeds her soul, honors her achievements, and gives her a solid base on which to fly to new heights.

"Her limit is set" takes on new meaning in the context of partnerships as a reminder to accept our roles as motivators of her empowerment and personal development. It is a promise to support her as she breaks norms, tests boundaries, and expands the frontiers of what is possible. We can open a universe of limitless possibilities—where her limit is actually no limit at all—through unshakable support, unconditional love, and unwavering faith in her potential.

WHAT SHE NEEDS, WHAT SHE WOULD LIKE...

"The colors that paint a vibrant relationship, where understanding and love intertwine to create a masterpiece of shared happiness, are what she needs and what she would like."

Understanding and meeting her needs and wants in the complex dance of relationships becomes an art of love, empathy, and intimate connection. A path of profound understanding, where her needs are satisfied with unflinching dedication and her wishes and aspirations are valued, awaits those who set out on this journey.

She requires a solid foundation upon which trust and security may be established, not just a few showy gestures. It is the certainty that her heart will be treasured, her feelings will be accepted, and her insecurities will be cradled tenderly. Knowing that her voice will be heard, her thoughts will be respected, and her dreams will be supported gives her comfort. It is the knowledge that she has a companion and is not alone. Beyond the requirements, she wants the delicate threads of happiness, surprise, and shared experiences to adorn the tapestry of love. Little things like a tender touch, a considerate act, or an unplanned experience serve as powerful reminders of how much she is loved and appreciated. Her preferences can be seen, heard, and respected thanks to the delicate dance of compromise and mutual discovery.

The secret to this great friendship is active listening and attempting to fully comprehend her on a personal and intimate level. It takes a sincere willingness to delve into the complexity of her ideas, feelings, and dreams, as well as a sincere interest. We close the gap between what she needs and what she wants by speaking with her in an empathic manner. understanding. But my own expertise is insufficient. The connection only really comes to life through the acts that result from this understanding. It entails making a concerted effort to attend to her needs, go above and above to satisfy her desires, and foster an environment where she can flourish. The dedication to continuously learn from and adjust to her changing needs and wants ensures that the love and care given remain ever-present.

Meeting her needs and giving her what she wants becomes a continual journey, a dance of development and shared learning, in the vast fabric of love. It is a call to continually seek out deeper comprehension, stronger bonds, and steadfast support. Taking care of this delicate balance allows us to develop a

So, we'll start this admirable endeavor of attending to her needs and granting her wishes. Let us learn to hear the beats of her heart, and let us, by our deeds, make a symphony of love and fulfillment. May we never forget that by appreciating and comprehending her needs and wants, we grow a relationship that goes beyond conventional bounds, blossoming into a remarkable voyage of shared delight and limitless potential.

WORK IT OUT

It is in the depths of our commitment that we learn the transforming power of togetherness and the limitless potential of our love. "When challenges arise, love prevails as we rise above, hand in hand, and work it out together."

There are times in the complex web of relationships when life's tides bring forth difficulties that put our bond to the test. The expression "work it out" assumes a profoundly significant meaning during these tough times—it serves as a call to action, a pledge to overcome challenges, and a reminder that love and determination are capable of overcoming any obstacle.

In a relationship, "working it out" is not a passive process; rather, it is an active quest for understanding, development, and resolution. It necessitates open communication, a readiness to hear and understand one another's viewpoints. It exhorts us to put the greater benefit of the relationship ahead of ego, pride, and self-interest. Being vulnerable and willing to share our hearts, anxieties, and uncertainties is a requirement for working things out. It calls for providing a space where both partners can express their emotions without fear of criticism or condemnation. By being vulnerable, we build stronger bonds that promote an atmosphere of closeness, trust, and emotional support. Working it out occasionally calls for flexibility and compromise. Finding a middle ground and looking for solutions that respect the wants and requirements of both parties is a delicate dance. It takes humility to admit our own failings and devotion to achieving win-win solutions that strengthen the connection. Working out a disagreement in the face of one takes tolerance and comprehension. Knowing that conflicts will inevitably arise but how we handle them will determine how strong our relationship is. It involves looking for a solution through polite discourse and a sincere desire to achieve harmony rather than through hostility or domination.

Working it out is building resilience, which is the ability to keep going in a relationship in the face of difficulty. It is an agreement to face challenges together while clinging to the conviction that love can outlast all obstacles. It entails accepting that obstacles present chances for development and that, with tenacity and one another's support, we can overcome them and emerge stronger and more unified than before.

Although working things out in relationships is not always easy, it is through these difficulties that we come to understand the transformative power of love. We discover secret depths in both ourselves and our partners during the process of figuring it out. We strengthen our bond, develop resiliency, and cultivate a love that goes beyond the ordinary through overcoming challenges.

Therefore, let's accept the invitation to "work it out" in our relationships. Let's approach problems with open minds and hearts, determined to build bridges of understanding and fan the flame of love. May we never forget that commitment, comprehension, and steadfast support provide the way to growth and enduring fulfillment. Together, we can overcome any challenge.

LOVE

"Love, the sacred thread that binds hearts, transcends space and time, igniting souls and illuminating the way to everlasting happiness in relationships."

Love has the capacity to alter, inspire, and uplift. Its timeless essence permeates the world of relationships. It is the mystical power that brings people together, bridging distances and creating a complex web of closeness.
We find a haven of vulnerability in the sacred realm of love, where souls entwine and find comfort in one another's presence. We experience a deep sense of purpose, commitment, and compassion when we fall in love. It is a power that inspires us to see below the surface, to treasure our partner's soul, and to promote their development and wellbeing. Love is an adventure that invites us to delve into the depths of our own hearts and the souls of those we love. It is a pledge to comprehend, cherish, and accept one another with all of our shortcomings. It is the decision to embrace vulnerability, to share our hopes and anxieties, and to create a link that is based on mutual respect and trust that will last forever. We learn that in the world of love, real power comes from compassionately empowering and uplifting our partners rather than from dominating or manipulating them. Love creates a secure environment where development

thrives—a place where we motivate one another to achieve greater heights, follow our passions, and realize our full potential. We are held in the arms of love. Love is a guiding light that helps us get through even the darkest of storms. When difficulties emerge, we must provide unwavering support, a kind touch to heal wounds, and genuine encouragement to build resilience. Love serves as a constant reminder that we have someone to lean on and with whom we can share our pleasures and sorrows in life.

Above all else, love is a gift that we give and receive and has the capacity to change our lives and the lives of the people we care about. It is a call to embrace openness, deepen connections, and take part in the indescribable beauty of shared experiences.

Therefore, let us accept love's gentle touch, fiery power, and limitless capacity for healing and upliftment. Let's create a love that goes beyond the commonplace, that becomes a beacon in our lives, and that imprints our spirits forever. Since love weaves hearts together in the arena of relationships, it gives our life purpose, joy, and the tremendous richness of shared existence.

There will inevitably be joyful and trying times along the path of love. Love however remains. Love endures adversity and the test of time with steadfastness. It is the decision to be present, to put money into something, and to constantly fan the flame that burns within our hearts.

LOVE AND PASSION

"Love and passion merge, forming a fiery symphony that fuels the depths of our souls, stokes desire, and paints the canvas of our relationships with vibrant hues of intimacy, connection, and everlasting bliss."

In the world of relationships, love and passion combine to form a timeless dance of ferocity and compassion. They serve as the foundation for the deep connection that develops between two people, a relationship that awakens desire, feeds it, and fills the shared journey with the vivacious hues of intimacy and uncontrolled happiness.
A soft thread that flows through the hearts of two people, love, the basis of relationships, ties them together in a web of loyalty and caring. The understanding that goes beyond words, the gentle touch that calms, and the everlasting support that inspires. Love creates a safe environment for vulnerability and genuine expression, nurturing and fostering a sense of security. The heartbeat of love is a passionate flame that dances within. The connection is electrified by uncontrolled, unbridled energy, which gives it a spirit of adventure and discovery. To ignite the depths of the soul and free the spirit, passion is the fire that feeds desire. It is an insatiable need for one another that can only be sated by the close fusion of bodies and hearts. Borders and restraints vanish in the dance of love and passion. A

symphony of private exchanges occurs between them, cementing their bond and establishing a shared language that goes beyond words. In a universe where time is suspended and only the present exists, love and passion arouse the senses and wrap two souls. A commitment to being totally present for one another and valuing every shared experience is the foundation of love and passion. They encourage thoughtful deeds, displays of affection, and fostering one's partner's particular wants and needs. The exploration of one another's bodies, brains, and souls is fostered by love and desire, building a deeper understanding that only strengthens the tie between two people.

But care and balance are necessary for love and passion. It is essential to moderate the heat of passion with the softness of love so that both partners have a sense of worth, deference, and adoration. Open communication is necessary for love and passion because it enables the expression of needs and limitations in a vulnerable and trusting way. This exquisite dance allows love and passion to coexist in perfect harmony. Love and passion transform into the forces that push the ordinary into the spectacular in the world of relationships. They give the voyage life, passion, and a sense of direction. Every encounter, touch, and display of affection is given life by love and passion, which serves as a reminder of the immense beauty and transformational power of human connection.

Consequently, let's embrace the age-old dance of passion and love in our relationships. Let us fan the flame within, relishing the intensity of desire while developing a love that is unwavering, kind, and compassionate. Creating a marriage where love and desire intersect, creating a symphony of shared bliss, and making every moment a tribute, may we navigate this beautiful balance with care and intention.

PRIVATE STUFF I MAKE

PERSONAL CONSIDERATIONS

In the pages of the insightful book "Man's Reflections," my own thought plays a crucial part in the area of relationships—an introspective trip that changes my interactions and fosters bonds based on empathy, respect, and authenticity. My own consideration acts as a compass in the tapestry of "Man's Reflections," directing how I interact with others in the area of relationships. It is a keen grasp of the effects my thoughts, feelings, and behavior have on people around me as well as a conscious awareness of my own ideas, feelings, and behaviors. I try to approach relationships with intention and integrity thanks to this self-awareness. My own perspective highlights the significance of empathy—the remarkable capacity to comprehend and share the feelings of others—in the book's narrative. It requires a sincere effort to pay close attention, to verify my partner's experiences, and to value their individual viewpoint. By encouraging empathy, I establish a secure environment where trust and understanding can grow, laying the groundwork for a profound and meaningful connection. A fundamental concept that guides all of my interactions in relationships, respect is a personal consideration I give in "Man's Reflections" that goes beyond empathy. It encourages me to respect my partner's autonomy, limitations, and uniqueness while acknowledging their intrinsic value and the benefits they offer to the partnership. I promote an atmosphere of equality through respect, building a relationship built on partnership.   Another important factor I personally take into account in partnerships is authenticity. It motivates me to present myself honestly, without pretense or masks. I make room for genuine connection by accepting vulnerability and honesty, enabling my partner to see and get to know the real me. I create an environment where trust and intimacy can flourish through authenticity, creating a strong sense of closeness. My own thought urges me to prioritize good communication within the context of "Man's Reflections." It serves as a reminder of the importance of active listening, honest expressing of feelings, and an impartial approach to resolving disputes. In order to cultivate a relationship that thrives on open and honest communication, I make sure that my partner feels heard, respected, and understood. My personal focus in the book's examination of relationships includes development and growth. It motivates me to support and promote my partner's individual journey in recognition of how personal growth strengthens our relationship. As we negotiate the ever-changing terrain of life together, it is a commitment to continuously learn, develop, and adapt.   In the end, "Man's Reflections," which depicts my own relationship considerations, acts as a compass—a direction—to cultivate relationships that are significant, respectful, and genuine. It motivates me to promote empathy, respect, authenticity, effective communication, and personal development in the context of relationships so that love can grow and the partnership can prosper.

My own reflection becomes a constant companion as "Man's Reflections" develops, serving as a reminder of the transformational potential of self-reflection and deliberate decisions in fostering profound and satisfying relationships. When personal concern becomes the cornerstone of our interactions with others, it is a testimonial to the depth of connection and the richness of experience that may be attained.